LIVING FOR CHRIST:

Resisting Temptation Using the Word of God

ERIC DIGGS

This book is copyrighted by Eric Diggs. Copyright © 2022. All rights reserved.

No part of this publication may be reproduced, stored in a retrieval system or transmitted in any way by any means, electronic, mechanical, photocopy, recording, or otherwise, without the prior permission of the author except as provided by USA copyright law.

Editing by Lisa Thompson at writebylisa@gmail.com

All Scripture quotations are from the ESV® Bible (The Holy Bible, English Standard Version®), copyright © 2001 by Crossway, a publishing ministry of Good News Publishers. Used by permission. All rights reserved.

Paperback: Digg that Publishing

E-book: Digg that Publishing

Contents

Introduction 1

Understanding Temptation 4

You Can't Do This in Your
Own Strength 8

Fighting Sinful Thoughts 11

Renew Your Mind 14

The Holy Spirit 18

Make Jesus Lord 21

The Way of Escape 26

Repentance 28

Close All Open Doors..32

Closing Remarks...34

Endnotes...36

Introduction

Do you find yourself struggling with the same sin? Do you find yourself in a vicious cycle of sinning and confessing? Are you tired of giving in to temptation? Do you wonder how you can win the fight against the biggest roadblocks in your Christian journey? If so, then this book is for you. In John 8:31–32, Jesus says, "If you abide in my word, you are truly my disciples, and you will know the truth, and the truth will set you free." In John 14:6, Jesus says, "I am the way, and the truth, and the life. No one comes to the Father except through me." And in John 8:36, Jesus says, "So if the Son sets you free, you will be free indeed." I want you to know that there is freedom in Jesus from whatever you are struggling with. There is nothing too big for God. In this book, I will teach you how to use the Word of God to consistently resist temptation.

Before we get into the deep content of this book, I want you to first change your mindset. Your new mindset going forward is this: Living holy and resisting temptation is not a streak—it is a lifestyle. Often, when we are fighting against any temptation, we tend to count the days, e.g., I haven't smoked a cigarette in twenty days and thirteen hours. Counting the days isn't bad, but when we start counting the days, we often get caught up in trying to keep the streak in our own strength, which more often than not leads to failure. When it comes to living a Christian lifestyle in general, you cannot do it in your own strength. In John 15:5, Jesus says, "I am the vine;

you are the branches. Whoever abides in me and I in him, he it is that bears much fruit, for apart from me you can do nothing." If you want to continue living a Christian lifestyle, you must stay connected to Jesus. (I will talk about this in more detail later in the book.)

Finally, before we get into the meat of this book, I want to remind you that you are not alone in this fight. First Peter 5:9 tells us to "Resist him [the devil], firm in your faith, knowing that the same kinds of suffering are being experienced by your brotherhood throughout the world." Christians all around the world are fighting this fight of faith. So keep your head up and stay encouraged.

Understanding Temptation

Before you can start resisting temptation, you must first understand what temptation is and where it comes from. According to the *Oxford Learner's Dictionary*, temptation can be defined as "the desire to do something, especially something wrong or unwise."[1] Now biblically speaking, James 1:13–14 says this about temptation: "Let no one say when he is tempted, 'I am being tempted by God,' for God cannot be tempted with evil, and he himself tempts no one. But each person is tempted when he is lured and enticed by his own desire." We can learn two key things from this passage of Scripture: God does not tempt us, and temptation comes from our own desires. We often blame God for what we go through, but it is not his fault. When you blame God, this keeps you from holding yourself accountable for your actions and desires. This will keep you from getting free because the first step to freedom is being honest, especially with yourself.

The next thing you must become aware of when it comes to fighting temptation is the key battleground: your mind. Every action starts with a thought. No one can do anything without first thinking about it. Each and every day, we all have thoughts. Some are good and some are bad. We cannot always control the thoughts that come into our heads. However, once a bad thought enters your mind, what you do with it is very important. Every time we have a thought, we are to judge whether the thought lines up with Jesus. So we ask, how do I know if Jesus is speaking to me or not? In John 10:27, Jesus says, "My sheep hear my voice, and I know them, and they follow me." We can judge if a thought lines up with Jesus if it agrees with what he taught, said, and did. In order to find out these things, we must read our Bible, and more specifically, the words of Christ. If you want to understand who Jesus is and what Jesus did, you must spend time with him.

When it comes to understanding temptation, be aware that you have an enemy. As believers, the devil is always trying his best to oppose us. You must be mindful of this because the easiest way to get taken out in a war is to not know you're in one to begin with. In John 10:10, Jesus says, "The thief comes only to steal and kill and destroy. I came that they may have life and have it abundantly." And then 1 Peter 5:8 says, "Be sober-minded; be watchful. Your adversary the devil prowls around like a roaring lion, seeking someone to devour." The devil is seeking someone to deceive. He is looking for someone to hold captive in bondage. However, if you are aware and alert, the devil will not be able to devour you.

You Can't Do This in Your Own Strength

The biggest thing you must understand when it comes to resisting temptation is that you cannot do it in your own strength. As a matter of fact, if you try to fight temptation in your own strength, you will eventually fail. If you are going to live a holy lifestyle, you need Jesus. In John 15:5, Jesus says, "I am the vine; you are the branches. Whoever abides in me and I in him, he it is that bears much fruit, for apart from me you can do nothing." Here, it becomes very clear that you cannot produce the fruit of Jesus in your life in your own strength. The analogy of a vine and a branch is very powerful. Think about this: If a branch is connected to a vine, then it can grow and produce fruit. However, if a branch becomes disconnected from the vine, then it can no longer grow and produce any fruit. Likewise, as long as we are connected to Jesus, we will produce his fruit in our lives. But the moment we get disconnected from Jesus is the moment we stop producing his fruit.

So the question becomes, what is the fruit of Jesus? Galatians 5:22–23 says, "But the fruit of the Spirit is love, joy, peace, patience, kindness, goodness, faithfulness, gentleness, self-control; against such things there is no law." If you want to produce this kind of fruit in your life, you must stay connected to Jesus daily. This is why it is so important to read your Bible, pray, and worship every day. How can you become like someone that you never spend any time with? In order to become more like Jesus, you must consistently spend quality time with him. The more time you spend with Jesus, the more he will teach you how to live a godly life.

Fighting Sinful Thoughts

If the key battleground for temptation is the mind, then what are you supposed to do when you get a sinful thought? Second Corinthians 10:5 says, "We destroy arguments and every lofty opinion raised against the knowledge of God, and take every thought captive to obey Christ." So when you get a sinful thought, you must immediately make it obey Christ. How do you do this? In Luke 10:19, Jesus says, "Behold, I have given you authority to tread on serpents and scorpions, and over all the power of the enemy, and nothing shall hurt you." As Christians, we are not victims in this life. Jesus did not leave us down here powerless. Through Jesus, we have authority over the devil. You use that authority through your words. The words you speak shape the world you live in. Proverbs 18:21 says, "Death and life are in the power of the tongue, and those who love it will eat its fruits."

So when it comes to fighting bad thoughts, you must speak to them and tell them to get out of your mind. Whenever I have a thought that goes against the teachings of Jesus, I point to my head and say, "I command this thought to leave my mind in Jesus's name. I will not think on this." The thought will leave immediately, but at times, the thought will come back. Whenever the thought comes back, speak to it again and command it to leave your mind in Jesus's name. Do this as many times as necessary. For example, if a tempting thought comes back in your mind twenty times a day, then you cast that thought out of your mind by using your words and the authority that Jesus gave you twenty times that day.

The worst mistake you can make when it comes to fighting bad thoughts is dwelling on a bad thought that is in your mind and not saying anything to it. Instead of speaking to a tempting thought, many people will often dwell on that thought. Remember, every action starts with a thought. So if I want to change the actions I am producing, I must change what I am thinking about. If I am constantly thinking about tempting thoughts and not telling them to get out of my mind in Jesus's name, then I will find myself constantly giving into temptation.

Renew Your Mind

Your biggest weapon when it comes to resisting temptation is the Word of God. In Ephesians 6:17, the Word of God is described as the sword of the Spirit. We must use this weapon to fight against temptation. If every action starts with a thought, then in order to produce the actions of God, we must first start thinking his thoughts. We do this by washing out or cleansing our old ways of thinking with his Word. Romans 12:2 tells us, "Do not be conformed to this world, but be transformed by the renewal of your mind, that by testing you may discern what is the will of God, what is good and acceptable and perfect." If you don't ever read your Bible, then you will never know the will of God. And if you don't know the will of God, then it will be impossible to live it out.

Renewing your mind is a continual process. You don't just do it once and then never do it again. You must do it daily. Romans 10:17 says, "So faith comes from hearing, and hearing through the word of Christ." Again, hearing is continual. We must consistently hear the words of Christ in order to keep them at the forefront of our minds. If you want to think the thoughts of Christ, you must read and speak his words continually. If you do this, you will begin to effortlessly produce the actions of Christ in your life. Once you understand what the will of God is, then you will also understand what goes against the will of God. Once you can recognize what goes against the will of God, you can use the words of God to speak his will. Simply put, you want to fill your mind with God's Word so that you will have something to combat anything that comes in your mind that is against God.

So read your Bibles! And if you don't know where to start, I recommend you start in the book of Matthew and read through the New Testament first. Many temptations come to take your focus away from Jesus. Once your focus is off Jesus and shifted to your problem, that leaves room for the devil to come in and discourage you. However, if you renew your mind continually, this will constantly keep your focus on Jesus, and Satan won't be able to have his way in your life. Also, I encourage you to find Scriptures that talk about the sins you struggle with and read those passages daily. For example, if you're struggling with lust, then you need to read Bible verses on sexual purity and holiness. If you're struggling with worry and depression, then you need to read Scriptures on peace and joy. If you're struggling with anger, then you need to read passages about self-control and patience. Whatever you're struggling with, read Bible verses on that topic every day. (Google is a great place to go to find the Scriptures you're looking for.) Jesus gives us an example of how to use the Word of God to resist temptation in Matthew 4:1–11. Here, the devil begins to tempt Jesus with the things of this world, but every time Jesus is tempted, he responds with, "It is written." So whenever you are tempted, you must respond to that thought with what the Word of God says about that topic.

The Holy Spirit

Jesus left us with the Holy Spirit to help us overcome life's daily struggles. Many Christians go their whole lives without understanding the role of the Holy Spirit in a believer. To start with, the Holy Spirit is a helper, and he helps us understand God's Word. In John 14:26, Jesus says, "But the Helper, the Holy Spirit, whom the Father will send in my name, he will teach you all things and bring to your remembrance all that I have said to you." The Holy Spirit bears witness about Jesus. In John 15:26, Jesus says, ""But when the Helper comes, whom I will send to you from the Father, the Spirit of truth, who proceeds from the Father, he will bear witness about me." The Holy Spirit shows us truth, things that are to come, and the things that are of Jesus. In John 16:13–15, Jesus again says, "When the Spirit of truth comes, he will guide you into all the truth, for he will not speak on his own authority, but whatever he hears he will speak, and he will declare to you the things that are to come. He will glorify me, for he will take what is mine and declare it to you. All that the Father has is mine; therefore I said that he will take what is mine and declare it to you." The Holy Spirit also gives us power and helps us to be witnesses for Christ. Acts 1:8 says, "But you will receive power when the Holy Spirit has come upon you, and you will be my witnesses in Jerusalem and in all Judea and Samaria, and to the end of the earth."

The Holy Spirit plays a pivotal role in helping us live a godly lifestyle daily. Galatians 5:16 tells us, "But I say, walk by the Spirit, and you will not gratify the desires of the flesh." Again, going back to the insight about not living this life in your own strength, Jesus did not leave us down here helpless. God gave us his Spirit to help us live out his nature. Whenever you are facing temptation, lean on the Holy Spirit to help you get through. That's why, every day, I say, "Holy Spirit, help me live for Christ."

Make Jesus Lord

Have you made Jesus the Lord of your life? Many Christians will allow Jesus to be their Savior, but not many Christians allow Jesus to be their Lord. When Jesus is the Lord of your life, then he becomes your master, which means he is the one who calls the shots and makes the decisions. If Jesus is not the Lord of your life, then that means you are the one making the decisions. And you must understand that you cannot ask God to change a life that you haven't given him authority over. In Luke 6:46, Jesus asks, "Why do you call me 'Lord, Lord,' and not do what I tell you?" If Jesus is truly the Lord of your life, then you will do what he says. Jesus wants all of you, not just a part of you.

So what does a life look like that is completely surrendered to Jesus? Well, in Luke 4:47–48, Jesus says this: "Everyone who comes to me and hears my words and does them, I will show you what he is like: he is like a man building a house, who dug deep and laid the foundation on the rock. And when a flood arose, the stream broke against that house and could not shake it, because it had been well built." When your life is completely surrendered to Jesus, you will do what he says. And when you do what he says, the storms of life will not be able to break you down. Temptation will not be able to make you give in. This is because you have a firm foundation that is built on the words of Christ.

But what does a life look like that is not completely surrendered to Jesus? Well, in Luke 6:49, Jesus says this: "But the one who hears and does not do them is like a man who built a house on the ground without a foundation. When the stream broke against it, immediately it fell, and the ruin of that house was great." When your life is not completely surrendered to Jesus, you will not do what he says. And when you don't do what he says, the storms of life will break you down. You will find yourself going in cycles. One day, you'll be resisting temptation, and the next day, you'll be going down a deep pit of giving in to temptation.

Everyone gets tempted, but only the words of Jesus can set you free and keep you free. However, you must allow Jesus to be the Lord of your life. You must allow him to tell you what to do, and then you must do it. If you do not, then you will struggle. Remember, you cannot live a holy lifestyle in your own strength, and the Word of God is your biggest weapon in this fight.

Remember that you can do all the reading of the Bible in the world, you can watch powerful sermons, you can read books that help strengthen your faith, but that all means nothing if you do not actually apply what you have learned in your life. James 1:22 says, "But be doers of the word, and not hearers only, deceiving yourselves." A big part of Jesus being the Lord of your life is hearing his words and doing them.

If you want to completely surrender your life to Christ to make him the Lord of your life, then pray this prayer out loud:

> Jesus, I surrender my life to you. I'm tired of doing things my way. I have come to realize that your way is better. Jesus, I cannot live holy in my own strength. I lean on you to show me how to live. Today, I choose to make you the Lord of my life. I repent of all my sins,

and I believe that you died on the cross just for me and God raised you from the dead on the third day. I thank you, Lord, that the same resurrection power is working in me and freeing me from all habitual sins. Amen.

The Way of Escape

God always provides a way of escape for us out of temptation. The problem is, most of the time, when you are tempted, you immediately focus on the temptation and on how strong it is. Instead, you should start focusing on seeking God for the way of escape each time. First Corinthians 10:13 says, "No temptation has overtaken you that is not common to man. God is faithful, and he will not let you be tempted beyond your ability, but with the temptation he will also provide the way of escape, that you may be able to endure it." This verse includes several key points. First, temptation is common to man. We all are tempted each and every day.

In addition, God will not allow us to be tempted beyond what we can bear. That means that although we all are tempted, there is always a way out. We never have to get stuck in any area. So start asking God for the way of escape each time you're tempted, and he will show you.

Repentance

James 1:12 says, "Blessed is the man who remains steadfast under trial, for when he has stood the test he will receive the crown of life, which God has promised to those who love him." Temptation is just a test, and when you pass it, you will be blessed. However, what do we do if we give into temptation?

Whenever you give into temptation, you will feel terrible, but instead of sitting around all day and sulking, you simply need to repent to get back on track. Whenever you sin, you want to repent and ask Jesus for forgiveness. True repentance means you make a 180-degree turn. That means you were going in one direction, but now you make a turn to go in another direction. But Christians often make a 360-degree turn instead. They start one way, then make a turn, and somehow end up back where they started. However, God sent Jesus to die on the cross and take away our sins and make a way for us so that we do not have to repeat those same cycles.

We must repent because when we sin, sin separates us from God. Our God is holy, and he cannot be where there is sin. When you repent, you admit to God that what you did was wrong, then you ask him for forgiveness. You should also ask Jesus to wash you and cleanse you in his blood and to teach you how not to do that sin again. Remember, we cannot fight temptation in our own strength. We must depend on Jesus to teach us how.

True repentance comes from the heart. When you don't truly repent from the heart, you will find yourself repeating a vicious cycle of sinning and confessing. This can be termed as worldly sorrow. (See 2 Corinthians 7:10.) However, when you have godly sorrow, you will repent from your heart. The biggest difference between godly sorrow and worldly sorrow is that worldly sorrow never produces the fruit of a changed life. When you have worldly sorrow, you will make excuses for why you keep falling into the same sins, but when you have godly sorrow, you will cry out from your heart to the Lord, admitting that you are wrong and you need his help. There is a difference between feeling guilty and sorry because you were caught and experienced the consequences of your sin versus truly feeling sorry because you understand God's heart and you don't want to hurt him.

Once you repent, you no longer have any need to feel condemned. Condemnation does not come from God. Romans 8:1 tells us, "There is therefore now no condemnation for those who are in Christ Jesus." Conviction, however, comes from the Holy Spirit, and that leads to repentance. The difference between conviction and condemnation is that when you feel condemned, you will feel ashamed and guilty. Repentance leads us to turn away from our sins, but guilt and shame leads to us going in cycles. Once we repent, we no longer need to feel ashamed and guilty. Whenever we repent, we can have confidence that God has forgiven us of our sins. First John 1:9 says, "If we confess our sins, he is faithful and just to forgive us our sins and to cleanse us from all unrighteousness."

Close All Open Doors

Another key to resisting temptation is closing all open doors. An open door is anything that leads to you giving in to the temptation. Some examples of open doors are TV shows, music, social media, and the people you hang around. What you watch and listen to and who you spend time with on a daily basis influences your thinking. And as was discussed earlier, your thinking influences your actions. For example, if I'm struggling with lust and I listen to songs that glorify sexual behaviors or if I watch shows that trigger sexual desires, then I will continue to struggle with lust. First Corinthians 15:33 tells us, "Do not be deceived: 'Bad company ruins good morals.'" Whenever you are hanging out with people, they're either influencing you or you're influencing them. You need to be aware of this.

In order to truly get free from a behavior, you must close all open doors. If you do not, then you will just continue to feed yourself more bad thoughts, leading to more temptations. You may be able to fight the temptation a couple times in your own strength, but the more you allow those tempting thoughts to penetrate your mind, the harder you will find it to continually resist temptation. Enough temptation already surrounds us, so why would you want to add to that by focusing on those thoughts?

Closing Remarks

You must understand that it is not bad to be tempted. However, what you do when you are tempted is very important. You must win the battle of the mind. Cast down all unclean thoughts. Read your Bible every day. Read about Jesus and what he taught, said, and did because the words of Christ are powerful. Find Scriptures that combat the specific issues you struggle with so that you can renew your mind with God's Word. Start confessing how you want to live every day. Life and death are in the power of the tongue, so speak things like, "Jesus has made me holy and righteous." Change your thoughts through your words so that you can change your actions. Worship the

Lord. In his presence, there is freedom. Never forget that you cannot resist temptation in your own strength. There's freedom in Jesus. There's strength in community. There's healing in confession. There's growth in accountability. There's wisdom in mentorship. There's peace in unity. So depend on Jesus every day to stay free, and surround yourself with a strong Christian community.

Galatians 6:9 says, "And let us not grow weary of doing good, for in due season we will reap, if we do not give up." Remember, resisting temptation is an everyday fight, so you must take it one day at a time. Living holy is not a streak; it's a lifestyle. The things you have learned in this short book work, but you must apply them every day to stay free. Don't ever become complacent. Stay on guard. I want to leave you with this final thought: If you're persistent, then you'll get it, but if you are consistent, then you'll keep it.

Endnotes

1 *Oxford Learner's Dictionary*, s.v. "temptation (*n.*)," accessed April 15, 2022, https://www.oxfordlearnersdictionaries.com/us/definition/american_english/temptation.

Made in the USA
Columbia, SC
19 October 2022